SPREAD
THE
HAGEL

SPREAD
THE
HAGEL

Jennifer Foster & Lianne Koster

SCRIPTUM

ISBN 978 94 6319 131 9

www.studiocookart.com
info@studiocookart.com
Instagram.com/studio_cookart
Facebook.com/cookartbook

www.scriptum.nl
info@scriptum.nl
Twitter.com/ScriptumNL
Facebook.com/UitgeverijScriptum

Preface

In 2014 we first met through our jobs. We soon discovered that we shared a passion for creative and innovative food: we had millions of ideas for dishes and the presentation of food. This was the beginning of Cookart, which involved experimenting with food; focusing on colour, shape, texture and styling. *Cookart, de kunst van het eten* was our first cookbook as a result of these experiments. In this period, a collaboration with De Pindakaaswinkel arose. After creating several recipes with peanut butter we quickly came to the conclusion: there is more to peanut butter than meets the eye. *Het Pindakaasboek* was the first book in which we concentrated on just one ingredient. Limiting yourself to one ingredient makes you more creative and the experiments yielded surprising combinations. *Spread the Hagel* is the successor to this. We wondered why a traditional Dutch sandwich spread that is so popular in the Netherlands, is hardly known abroad. *Spread the Hagel* has shown us that it does not just serve as a sandwich topping. Combinations such as sprinkles with bacon, gorgonzola or gingerbread have produced delicious and surprising recipes, making it possible to eat sprinkles throughout the day. Just like the men of Hagelswag, we want to make chocolate sprinkles known worldwide. In our book you will find traditional dishes from the Netherlands, but also traditional dishes from various other countries in which chocolate sprinkles are integrated. *Spread the Hagel!*

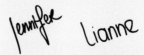

INDEX

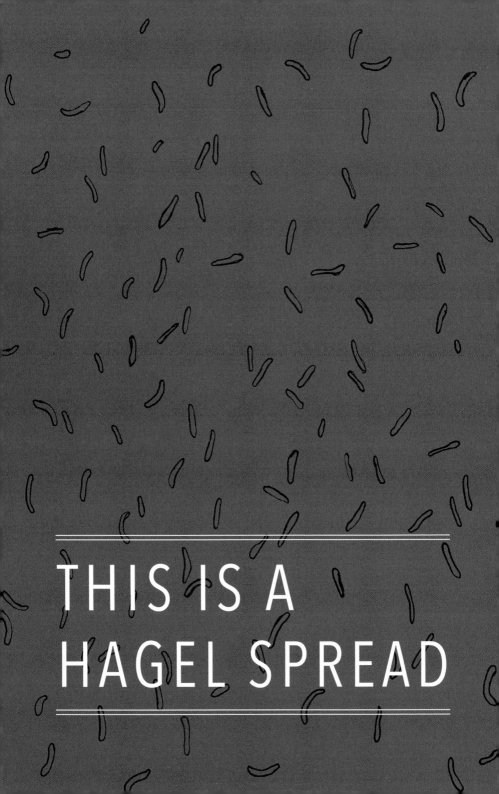

THIS IS A
HAGEL SPREAD

The history of
hagelslag

Most Dutch people cannot imagine that there was once a time when chocolate sprinkles did not exist. The sprinkles have been around for so long, it's hard to believe they haven't always been here. Sprinkles do not grow on trees and they aren't real mouse drops[1]. Who invented these sprinkles?

There are different theories about the history and the inventor of chocolate sprinkles. For example, the director of the candy manufacturer Venco is thought to have invented chocolate sprinkles around 1919. On a bleak autumn day, while watching the hail falling from the skies, director B.E. Dieperink came up with the idea of hagel (hail). This was the birth of white sprinkles with aniseed flavour as a sandwich spread – and it turned out to be a great success.

→

[1] In Belgium, hagelslag is also called mouse droppings.

....

Another legend tells the story of Hendrik de Vries, who started a wholesale trade in chocolate and confectionery in Amsterdam in 1890, called Venz. In 1936 the son of Hendrik, Gerard, came up with chocolate sprinkles – inspired by letters he had received from a five-year-old boy named H. Bakker. The boy had begged for chocolate as a topping for bread. Gerard is said to have spent many evenings in his kitchen, experimenting with ways to make the perfect, shiny sprinkles. Venz admits not knowing exactly whether this is correct, but it remains a beautiful legend.

Before the founding of Venz, De Ruijter was also in the bread-decorating business. In 1860 they started with the production and sale of so-called 'birth mice'. These were sugared anise seeds that were later sold in crushed form, under the name 'crushed mice' – or 'gestampte muisjes'. In the 1920s the demand for sweet toppings for bread increased – leading to the development of fruit-flavoured hagel, aniseed-flavoured hagel and anise cubes. The fruit-flavoured hagel was made in the flavours lemon, raspberry, orange and aniseed. In 1955 chocolate flakes were added and in 1957 the chocolate sprinkles were part of their assortment.

We cannot say with certainty who the inventor is of chocolate sprinkles. But that does not really matter, because it is here and we love it!

....

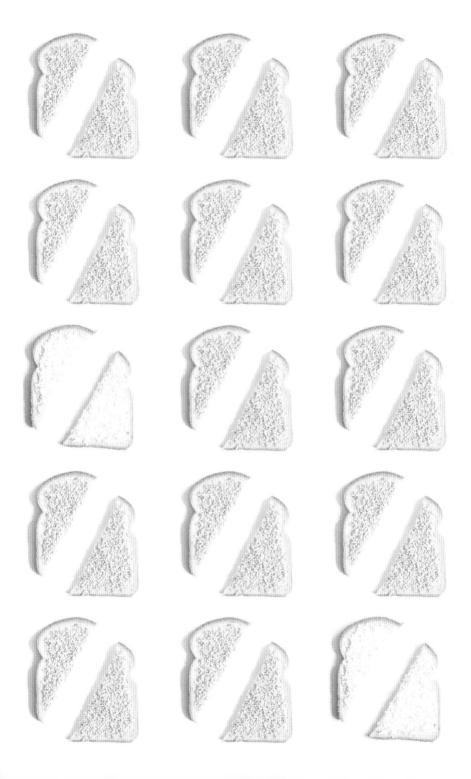

Making **hagel**slag

In the Netherlands you can get a package of sprinkles in every super-market, but unfortunately this is not the case outside this country. Making hagelslag yourself is the solution to this problem! You can easily make the most delicious sprinkles yourself. To make them shiny, hard and crunchy, the chocolate must first be tempered. You can read how this is done here:

Use small pieces of chocolate, like chocolate drops or chocolate which is broken into small pieces. Melt two thirds of the chocolate au bain marie. Once the chocolate has melted, remove the bowl from the heat source and add the remaining pieces of chocolate while stirring. Keep stirring until you have a nice homogeneous mass.

Depending on the amount of cocoa butter in the chocolate, each type of chocolate (dark, milk, white) requires a different temperature: dark chocolate requires melting to 50°C, milk to 45°C and white chocolate to a maximum of 43°C. The temperature of the dark chocolate combined with one third of the remaining chocolate should reach 31-32°C, milk should be 30-31°C and white chocolate 27-28°C.

Has the chocolate melted up to the required temperature? Pour the chocolate into a squeeze bottle or piping bag. Place a sheet of parchment paper horizontally on the counter. Squeeze out a thin and long line on the longest width of the sheet. Repeat this step until your entire sheet of parchment paper is covered with long thin strips. Allow the chocolate to harden and cool in a cool and dry place. Do you want to speed up this process? You can also place it in the fridge. Has the chocolate cooled down? The strips can be cut in shorter pieces by a sharp knife. Keep the sprinkles in a cool and dry place.

Funny **hagel**

Do you think that your slice of bread with chocolate sprinkles could use a boost? There are many types of sprinkles with small chocolate figures called funnies in the supermarket, but... you can also make these funnies yourself! To make these funnies you need a mould. You can choose to buy a ready-made mould or you can make an original mould yourself. Use food-safe materials, such as culinary silicone.

RECIPE: Melt chocolate as described on page 12. Pour into the mould of your choice and let it cool in a cool, dark place.

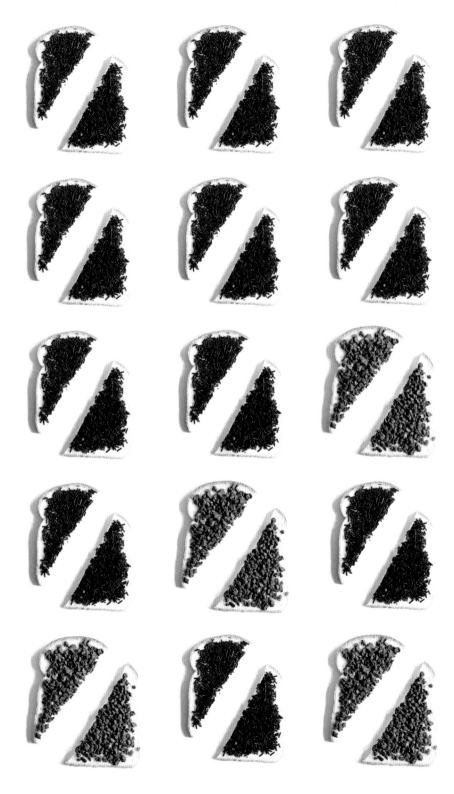

Putting quality back in **hagel**

....

From hagelslag to Hagelswag

Did you know that the Dutch tradition of chocolate as a bread topping is older than chocolate sprinkles? The exact start of this tradition is unclear, but we do know that after the First World War, when the price of sugar and cocoa – the most important ingredients of chocolate – dropped, chocolate on bread became popular. In addition to the Netherlands, Belgium, Denmark, France and even the Philippines have a tradition of eating chocolate with their breakfast. But the way the Dutch eat it, shaved or crumbled chocolate from the bar, is unique in the world.

Sprinkles on the other hand originated as a sugar spread, often with aniseed as a seasoning. According to the team of Hagelswag, it was not until 1936 that skimmed cocoa powder was added to the sugar spread for the first time, leading to the creation of sprinkles as we still know them today. Due to the popularity of chocolate sprinkles, real quality chocolate has almost disappeared from the Dutch breakfast table.

....

In 2016, Lennart de Jong and Robbert Vos started a crowdfunding campaign to share the best breakfast tradition in the Netherlands with the rest of the world. **Hagelswag** – a word joke of course – is a topping made of 100% real quality chocolate and the aim was for it to conquer the hearts (and mouths) of gourmets around the world. It worked! From Japan to the US, orders for Hagelswag poured in and within two weeks the men had collected enough money to share their chocolates with people all over the world.

Hagelswag is now widely available in various stores and supermarkets in the Netherlands, and also beyond. People from more than fifty countries have already become acquainted with our Dutch tradition. With Hagelswag, real chocolate has been given a place on breakfast tables worldwide.

Sprinkly granola

Preparation 10 minutes **Oven** 25 minutes

6-8 servings

INGREDIENTS

100 GR OAT FLAKES

3 TBSP PUMPKIN SEEDS

75 GR MIXED UNSALTED NUTS

2 TBSP COCONUT OIL

2 BIG TBSP HONEY

2 TSP CINNAMON

1 TSP GINGERBREAD SPICES

50 GR HAGELSWAG (HAGELSLAG)

EXTRA

MIXING BOWL

SAUCEPAN

BAKING PAPER

Preheat the oven to 160°C. Melt the coconut oil in a saucepan. Chop the nuts into rough pieces. Put the oatmeal, pumpkin seeds and nuts into a mixing bowl. Add the melted coconut oil and mix well. Then add the honey, cinnamon, gingerbread spices and hagelslag. Stir them in thoroughly. Cover the baking tray with baking paper and spread the granola mixture onto it.

Bake in the oven for 20-25 minutes, mixing it occasionally. Ready? Let it cool for 10 minutes.

TIP Do you use Hagelswag? Add it after baking the granola.

Breakfast muffins

Preparation 15 minutes **Oven** 20 minutes
12 muffins

INGREDIENTS

100 GR SPELT FLOUR
100 GR WHOLE GRAIN FLOUR
50 GR OATMEAL + A HANDFUL
FOR GARNISHING
20 GR GRATED COCONUT
2 TSP BAKING POWDER PINCH
OF SALT
1½ TSP CINNAMON
1 TSP BAKING SODA
2 EGGS
100 GR GREEK YOGHURT
100 ML MILK
50 ML RAPESEED OIL
75 GR HONEY
100 GR RASPBERRIES AND
BLUEBERRIES
80 GR COCONUT-HAZELNUTS-
HAGELSWAG (HAGELSLAG)
BAKING SPRAY

OPTIONAL: CREAM CHEESE

EXTRA

BAKING TRAY FOR 12 MUFFINS
2 MIXING BOWLS

Preheat the oven to 185°C. Mix all dry ingredients except the Hagelswag in a large mixing bowl and put this to the side. Beat the eggs in another bowl. Add the Greek yoghurt, milk, honey and rapeseed oil and mix well. Add this mixture to the dry ingredients, stirring as you do so. Stir in the hagelslag and raspberries and blueberries. Spoon the mixture into the greased baking tray. Garnish the muffins by sprinkling some oatmeal over them. Place in the oven for 20 minutes. Ready? Let the muffins cool off a bit and serve with cream cheese.

Overnight hail oats

Preparation 10 minutes **Wait** 1 night

1 serving

INGREDIENTS
35 GR OATMEAL

210 ML MILK

2 TBSP COCOA

1 TBSP SUGAR

½ TSP VANILLA EXTRACT

TOPPING:

HAGELSWAG (HAGELSLAG),
BANANA, HAZELNUT PIECES,
BLUEBERRIES, WHATEVER YOU
PREFER

EXTRA
MEASURING CUP

BLENDER

SAUCEPAN

Put all the ingredients (except the toppings) in
the blender jug. Stir or shake it together and
leave this in the fridge overnight.
The next morning blend the mixture into a
smooth substance. Heat this in a saucepan and
stir continuously until it becomes a firm porridge.
Once heated, put it in a bowl and decorate with
the toppings. Don't forget the hagelslag!

Dutch toast

Preparation 12 minutes

2 servings

INGREDIENTS

2 EGGS

200 ML CHOCOLATE MILK

6 SLICES OF WHITE BREAD

1½ TBSP BUTTER

HAGELSWAG (HAGELSLAG)

EXTRA

DEEP BOWL

FRYING PAN

Mix the eggs with the chocolate milk in a bowl.
Lay each slice of bread in the mixture, turning
them over and letting the mixture soak in well.
Heat the butter in a frying pan and cook the
slices for about 2.5 minutes on both sides. Put
the French toast on two plates and sprinkle
Hagelswag on top.

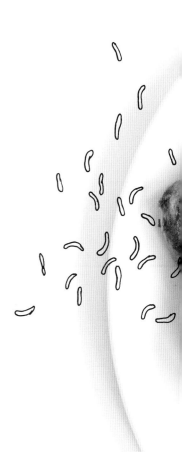

Hagel waffles

Preparation 15 minutes

6-8 servings

INGREDIENTS

400 GR SELF-RAISING FLOUR

1 TBSP BAKING POWDER

PINCH OF SALT

2 EGGS

150 GR SUGAR

100 ML OIL

375 ML MILK

1 PACKET OF VANILLA SUGAR

80 GR HAGELSLAG

BAKING SPRAY

EXTRA

MIXING BOWL

WAFFLE IRON

Mix together all the dry ingredients, except for the hagelslag. Gradually stir in the wet ingredients until well mixed. The hagelslag can then be stirred in. Switch on the waffle iron and spray it with baking spray. Use 1 to 1½ soup spoons of batter for each waffle. Bake the waffles and spray the waffle iron between waffles. Eat the waffles while they are still warm. They are delicious with ice cream!

Chocolate swirl rolls

Preparation 20 minutes **Oven** 15 minutes **Wait** 120 minutes

18 rolls

INGREDIENTS

7 GR OF DRIED YEAST
250 ML LUKEWARM MILK
2 TBSP SUGAR
75 GR BUTTER
1 EGG
PINCH OF SALT
450 GR FLOUR + SOME EXTRA
BAKING SPRAY
40 GR BROWN SUGAR
25 GR GRANULATED SUGAR
75 GR SOFTENED BUTTER
50 GR HAGELSLAG

TOPPING:
100 GR CREAM CHEESE
100 GR POWDERED SUGAR
1 TBSP MILK
1 TBSP VANILLA EXTRACT
2 TBSP SOFTENED BUTTER

EXTRA

MIXING BOWL
MIXER
BAKING PAPER
PLASTIC FOIL

Let the yeast dissolve in the lukewarm milk. Then add the sugar, salt, butter, egg and about half of the flour. Gradually mix this together with a mixer with a bread dough hook (or knead by hand). Continue adding in the flour until you have a nice soft dough. Knead for about 7-10 minutes. Scrape the dough off the sides of the bowl and pour 1 tbsp of vegetable oil around the sides of the bowl. Turn the dough over in the bowl so that it is covered with oil. Cover the bowl with cling film and allow it to rise in a warm place until it doubles in size.

Mix the sugars in a small bowl. Once the dough has risen, sprinkle flour on a worktop and turn out the dough onto the flour. Push the dough down so that it can then be rolled into a large rectangle. Spread the softened butter evenly over the dough and sprinkle the mixed sugars on top of the butter followed by the hagelslag. Starting on the long side, roll the dough up into a rolled log. Cut this up into slices about 2.5 cm thick and place these on a baking paper covered baking tray with enough space between them to double in size. Allow the rolls to sit for about an hour or until they have doubled in size.

Preheat the oven to 175°C. When the rolls have risen, bake for 15 minutes or until lightly browned. Then remove from the oven and allow to cool. Combine all the icing ingredients in a bowl and mix until smooth. Once the rolls are cool, drizzle icing on top and enjoy.

Confetti bruschetti

Preparation 10 minutes **Oven** 12 minutes

10 servings

INGREDIENTS
1 CIABATTA
5 TBSP OLIVE OIL
5 FIGS
100 GR GORGONZOLA
2 TBSP BALSAMIC VINEGAR
3 TBSP HONEY
3 TBSP DARK HAGELSLAG FLAKES

EXTRA
BAKING PAPER
BOWL

Preheat the oven to 200°C. Cut off the ends of the ciabatta. Cut the remainder of the ciabatta into 10 equal slanted slices. Sprinkle a little olive oil over the top of the slices and toast for 6 minutes in the oven. Remove the stalks from the figs and cut the figs into 8 slices. Distribute them over the ciabatta slices and put the gorgonzola on top.

Return to the oven until the gorgonzola has melted. Present the bruschetta with hagelslag as a topping.

Mix the honey with the balsamic vinegar in a bowl. Serve separately as a dressing.

Cheesy summer

Preparation 30 minutes **Wait** 6.5 hours

10 servings

INGREDIENTS

BASE:
200 GR DIGESTIVE BISCUITS
70 GR BUTTER
BAKING SPRAY

FILLING:
6 SHEETS OF GELATINE
6 TBSP WATER
750 GR STRAWBERRY QUARK
(OR CREAMY YOGHURT)
60 GR DARK HAGELSLAG

TOPPING:
200 GR STRAWBERRIES
2 SHEETS OF GELATINE
2 TBSP WATER

EXTRA

BAKING MOULD Ø20 CM
BAKING PAPER
BLENDER
MIXING BOWL
BOWL
SAUCEPAN

Cover the bottom of a 20 cm baking mould with baking paper. Break the biscuits into rough pieces and grind finely in the blender. Melt the butter in a pan and mix it together with the biscuits in a mixing bowl. Spray the baking form and put the mixture on the bottom, pressing it in firmly with the back of a spoon. Place the baking form in the fridge for half an hour. Soak the gelatine sheets in a bowl of cold water for 5 minutes, then squeeze them out and heat 6 tbsp of water in a saucepan. Add the gelatine and stir until it has dissolved. Put the strawberry quark in a bowl and add the gelatine mixture and hagelslag. Mix thoroughly. Take the baking mould out of the fridge and pour the gelatine mixture into it. Make the surface nice and smooth and leave in the fridge for at least 3 hours. Ready? For the topping, puree the strawberries in the blender. Soak the gelatine sheets in a bowl of cold water for 5 minutes. Squeeze them out and heat 2 tbsp of water in a saucepan. Add the gelatine and stir until it has dissolved. Add this to the strawberry mixture and mix thoroughly. Take the cheesecake out of the fridge and pour the strawberry mixture onto it. Again, place it in the fridge for at least 3 hours.

Spice up my life

Preparation 10 minutes

10 little balls

INGREDIENTS

1 X 1 CM GINGER

15 MEDJOUL DATES

2 TBSP GRATED COCONUT

2 TBSP SALTED PEANUTS

3 TBSP PUFFED RICE

2 TBSP DARK HAGELSLAG

EXTRA

GRATER

BLENDER

BOWL

Grate the ginger. Put this in a bowl with the pitted dates, coconut and peanuts. Grind with the blender and then add the puffed rice and hagelslag. Is it well mixed? Then knead the mixture and roll into balls before placing them in the fridge until you are ready to serve.

TIP Try this recipe with dark hagelslag with sea salt.

Bacon **hagel** cookies

Preparation 15 minutes **Oven** 25 minutes
Approximately 12 cookies

INGREDIENTS
90 GR BACON CUBES
80 GR UNSALTED BUTTER
80 GR SUGAR
1 EGG
80 GR FLOUR
PINCH OF SALT
75 GR HAGELSLAG

EXTRA
SAUCEPAN
KITCHEN PAPER
MIXING BOWL
MIXER
BAKING PAPER

Preheat the oven to 160°C. First bake the bacon cubes and let them dry off on kitchen paper. Put the softened butter, sugar, egg, flour and pinch of salt in a bowl and mix well. Then add the hagelslag and bacon cubes and mix them through. Cover a baking tray with baking paper. Use a spoon or ice scoop to make biscuits that are all about the same size. Don't place the biscuits too close to each other, as they will expand. Bake the biscuits for about 20-25 minutes in a preheated oven. Let the biscuits cool off on a cooling rack.

Crispy **hagel**

Preparation 10 minutes **Oven** 30 minutes

1 bowl

INGREDIENTS

1 TIN OF CHICKPEAS (240 GR
DRAINED WEIGHT)

1 TSP CUMIN

1 TSP GARLIC POWDER

LARGE PINCH OF CAYENNE PEPPER

1 TBSP WALNUT OIL

PINCH OF SALT

HANDFUL OF DARK CHOCOLATE
HAGELSLAG FLAKES

EXTRA

BAKING PAPER

COLANDER

KITCHEN TOWEL

BOWL

Preheat the oven to 200°C. Put the chickpeas in a colander and rinse well. Dab them dry with a kitchen towel and put them in a bowl and mix well with the oil and spices. Spread the chickpeas on the baking tray lined with baking paper and place in the oven for about 30 minutes. Stir occasionally. Done? Leave them to cool. Sprinkle with salt and hagelslag flakes.

Bacon strips

Preparation 25 minutes **Wait** 60 minutes

12 servings

INGREDIENTS

12 STRIPS OF BACON

1 BAR DARK CHOCOLATE

HAGELSLAG AS TOPPING

EXTRA

FRYING PAN

KITCHEN TOWEL

SAUCEPAN

OVEN-PROOF BOWL

Put some strips of bacon in the frying pan. Place the frying pan on medium heat. Turn the bacon as it begins to curl. Fry the other side until the bacon is nice and crisp. Dab the bacon strips dry on both sides with kitchen towel. Repeat until all the bacon strips are done.

Melt the dark chocolate on a low heat au bain marie. Stir well all the time. Cover part of the bacon strips with chocolate, using a spoon. Decorate the chocolate with hagelslag as topping. Place in the fridge for 60 minutes to cool.

INGREDIENTS

180 GR FLOUR

1 TSP BAKING SODA

½ TSP BAKING POWDER

½ TSP SALT

3 LARGE BANANAS (400 GR)

2 EGGS

125 GR GREEK YOGHURT

2 TBSP HONEY

40 GR LIGHT BROWN SUGAR

½ TSP VANILLA EXTRACT

40 GR HAGELSLAG

BAKING SPRAY

EXTRA

BAKING TIN

2 LARGE MIXING BOWLS

Banana bread

Preparation 15 minutes **Oven** 60 minutes
10 servings

Preheat the oven to 175°C. Mix the flour, baking soda, baking powder and salt together in a bowl and then put this aside. Mash up the bananas and put them in another mixing bowl. Would you prefer to have more of the banana's texture in your banana bread? Then mash up only two of the bananas and add the other banana in somewhat larger chunks. Add the eggs, Greek yoghurt, honey, brown sugar and a dash of vanilla extract to the banana mixture, and mix together carefully, but thoroughly. Finally add the hagelslag and mix thoroughly. Spray the baking tin well and pour in the banana mixture. Place it in the oven for 50-60 minutes. It is ready when a skewer comes out clean. You may need to cover the cake with tin foil after 45 minutes to prevent the cake from getting too brown. Leave the banana bread to cool.

Brown(cook)ie

Preparation 10 minutes **Oven** 10 minutes **Wait** 30 minutes
15-20 cookies

INGREDIENTS

150 GR BROWN DEMERARA SUGAR
110 GR SOFT BUTTER
1 EGG
1 TSP VANILLA EXTRACT
35 GR COCOA
125 GR FLOUR
½ TSP BAKING POWDER
½ TSP SALT
80 GR HAGELSLAG

EXTRA

2 MIXING BOWLS
1 BOWL
MIXER
BAKING PAPER

Preheat the oven to 175°C. Put the butter and sugar in a bowl and mix lightly. Add the egg and mix thoroughly. Finally add the vanilla extract. In another bowl mix the cocoa, flour, baking powder and salt together. Then add this to the other mixture and create a nice dough. Place this in the fridge for half an hour. Prepare a bowl with hagelslag. Use a teaspoon to scoop out small balls from the dough and roll together in your hands. Dip the ball in the hagelslag so that half the ball is covered. Cover a baking tray with baking paper and place the dipped balls on it with the hagelslag side facing upwards. Don't place the balls too close together. Bake for 10 minutes in the oven. Leave the biscuits to cool before eating.

Granola bars

Preparation 10 minutes **Oven** 35 minutes
10-12 bars

INGREDIENTS

2 TBSP WALNUT OIL
2 TBSP CHUNKY PEANUT BUTTER
3 TBSP HONEY
175 GR OATMEAL
75 GR APPLE SAUCE
ZEST OF ½ LEMON
100 GR APPLE (GRANNY SMITH)
1 EGG
50 GR PISTACHIO NUTS
3 DATES
5 TBSP HAGELSLAG MIX

EXTRA

BAKING TIN APPROX. 20 X 20 CM
BAKING PAPER
MIXING BOWL
SAUCEPAN

Preheat the oven to 180°C. Line the baking tin with baking paper. Heat the walnut oil, peanut butter and honey in a saucepan until it is properly mixed. Put the oatmeal in a mixing bowl and add the apple sauce and zest of the lemon. Peel the Granny Smith apples and cut into small pieces. Fold the apple and 3 tbsp of hagelslag through the oatmeal, and then add the honey mixture. Add an egg to the oatmeal and stir it well. The batter should be quite thick and firm. Cut the pistachios into rough pieces and add them to the batter, followed by the dates. Spoon the batter into the baking tin. Sprinkle the remaining 2 tbsp of hagelslag mix over the batter and press together well with the back of a spoon. Place the baking tin in the oven for 35 minutes, allowing it to bake and become a nice golden brown. Check it every 10 minutes. You may need to cover it with aluminium foil after 20 minutes to prevent it from becoming too brown. Done? Let it cool off before you cut it in slices.

Hagel dip
cookie dough

Preparation 5 minutes

Full bowl for dips

INGREDIENTS

40 GR SOFT BUTTER

160 GR CREAM CHEESE

1½ TSP VANILLA EXTRACT

60 GR WHITE DEMERARA
SUGAR

60 GR CASTER SUGAR

40 GR HAGELSLAG

EXTRA

BOWL

Mix everything, except the chocolate hagel, into a smooth mixture. Then add the hagelslag and stir it in. Tasty as a dip.

TIP Combine with the brioche on page 126.

Hagel fudge

Preparation 20 minutes **Wait** 60 minutes
Approximately 40 servings

INGREDIENTS

1 TIN CONDENSED MILK
350 GR WHITE CHOCOLATE
50 GR BUTTER
100 GR BROWN DEMERARA SUGAR
150 GR FLOUR
1 TSP CORNSTARCH
2 TSP VANILLA EXTRACT
PINCH OF SALT
70 GR DARK HAGELSLAG

EXTRA

BAKING TIN 20 X 15 CM
SAUCEPAN
BAKING PAPER

Line the baking tin with baking paper. Put the condensed milk, white chocolate, butter and brown sugar in a saucepan on low heat. Keep stirring well until the butter and chocolate have melted and all the ingredients are thoroughly mixed. Turn the heat down and add the flour, corn starch, vanilla extract and a pinch of salt. Stir until it is all mixed together. Pour the mixture into the baking tin and make sure that it is spread equally. Sprinkle the hagelslag over the top and allow to cool in the fridge for at least an hour.

Hagel balls

Preparation 15 minutes **Wait** 65 minutes

18 balls

INGREDIENTS
200 GR CREAM CHEESE
100 GR 75% CHOCOLATE
ZEST OF 1 ORANGE
BOWL WITH HAGELSLAG

EXTRA
SAUCEPAN
BOWL

Heat the cream cheese until it's hot. Break the chocolate into small pieces and put it in a bowl with the zest of orange. Pour in the cream cheese and let it rest for 5 minutes. Mix with a spoon. The chocolate should have melted completely. Place it in the fridge to cool.

After about an hour you can start making balls, using the mixture. Roll them in a bowl of hagelslag of choice until they are covered. These hagel balls are best eaten cold.

Brownie cake

Preparation 20 minutes **Oven** 25 minutes **Wait** 2 x 1.5 hours

16 servings

INGREDIENTS
175 GR BUTTER + SOME EXTRA
200 GR DARK CHOCOLATE
3 EGGS
275 GR CASTER SUGAR
50 GR COCOA
90 GR FLOUR
75 GR WHITE XL HAGEL

300 GR CREAM CHEESE
1 SMALL PACKET VANILLA SUGAR
1½ TBSP LEMON JUICE
100 GR POWDERED SUGAR
200 GR GREEK YOGHURT
250 GR CREAM
2 PACKETS DR. OETKER WHIP IT
100 GR CHOCOLATE FLAKES

EXTRA
SQUARE BAKING TIN
BAKING PAPER
PAN
OVEN PROOF BOWL
BATTER SPOON
MIXER
MIXING BOWLS

Cover the base of the baking tin with baking paper and then grease the baking tin. Melt the dark chocolate with the butter au bain marie. Once it has all melted, remove the pan from the heat and allow the chocolate to cool. In the meantime the convection oven should be preheated to 160°C. Mix the eggs and sugar together for about 5 minutes until thoroughly mixed and creamy. Once the chocolate mixture has cooled, this can be folded into the egg mixture with a batter spoon. Try to keep as much air in the mixture as possible. Add the cocoa and flour. Once this has become a homogeneous mixture, mix in the super hagel and spoon into the baking tin. Bake for 25 minutes. Once ready it should cool off in the baking tin.

For the topping, mix the cream cheese, vanilla sugar, lemon juice, powdered sugar and Greek yoghurt together. Mix the cream and whip it in another bowl and then add in the other mixture until it all becomes stiff. The chocolate flakes can be mixed in and the mixture then spooned in on top of the cooled brownie base. Place this in the fridge to cool thoroughly. Decorate with sprinkles if you like.

Chocolate hummus

Preparation 20 minutes

1 dip

INGREDIENTS

140 GR CANNED CHICKPEAS,
DRAINED
70 GR APPLE SAUCE
2 TBSP MAPLE SYRUP
½ TSP VANILLA EXTRACT
15 GR COCOA
1 TSP CINNAMON
2 TBSP HAGELSLAG

EXTRA

BLENDER

Start by removing the skin from the chickpeas. With a little care you can squeeze them out of their skins. It is a bit of work, but it does make the dip a lot smoother. Then put all the ingredients (except the hagelslag) in the blender and blend, to make a smooth mixture. Now you can mix in the hagelslag by hand.

TIP This dip is delicious with the cinnamon bites on page 64.

Cinnamon bites

Preparation 5 minutes **Wait** 16 minutes

24 triangles

INGREDIENTS
HALF LAVASH BREAD (170 GR)
60 GR BUTTER
100 GR GRANULATED SUGAR
2 LARGE TSP CINNAMON

EXTRA
SAUCEPAN
BAKING PAPER
PLATE

Preheat the oven to 190°C. Cut the halved bread into 3 slices. Every slice will be divided into 4 squares. Cut each square diagonally. Melt the butter in the bowl. Mix the granulated sugar with the cinnamon on the plate. Spread butter on both sides of the triangles and then lay them in the cinnamon sugar. Place the triangles on the baking tray covered with baking paper and allow the cinnamon bites to become crisp in the oven for about 16 minutes. Turn the triangles halfway through.

Serve these bites with the chocolate hummus of page 62.

Marshmallow dip

Preparation 15 minutes **Wait** 60 minutes

12 bites

INGREDIENTS

100 GR DARK CHOCOLATE

12 MARSHMALLOWS

HAGELSLAG OF YOUR CHOICE
AS TOPPING

EXTRA

SAUCEPAN

OVEN-PROOF BOWL

PLATE

Melt the dark chocolate au bain marie. Dip one side of the marshmallows in the chocolate and then roll them in the hagelslag topping of your choice. Sprinkle a little hagelslag over any chocolate that shows. Press the hagelslag down a little and put the marshmallows on a plate with the marshmallow side down. Refrigerate for 60 minutes.

Hagel bars

Preparation 15 minutes **Wait** 180 minutes

1 bar

INGREDIENTS

120 GR CHOCOLATE
TOPPINGS LIKE HAGELSLAG,
GRATED COCONUT, NUTS
BAKING SPRAY

EXTRA

2 SAUCEPANS
2 OVEN PROOF BOWLS
SILICONE CHOCOLATE BAR MOULD

Break the chocolate bar into pieces and melt au bain marie. **Tip**: for the perfect temperature look on page 12. When using two types of chocolate, melt separately. Spray the mould. Place the toppings onto the silicone mould. Has the chocolate melted? Pour it into the silicone mould and make sure it is evenly spread. Allow the chocolate to harden and cool in a cool and dry place. Do you want to speed up this process? You can also place it in the fridge.

TIP Silicone moulds can be found on www.studiocookart.com

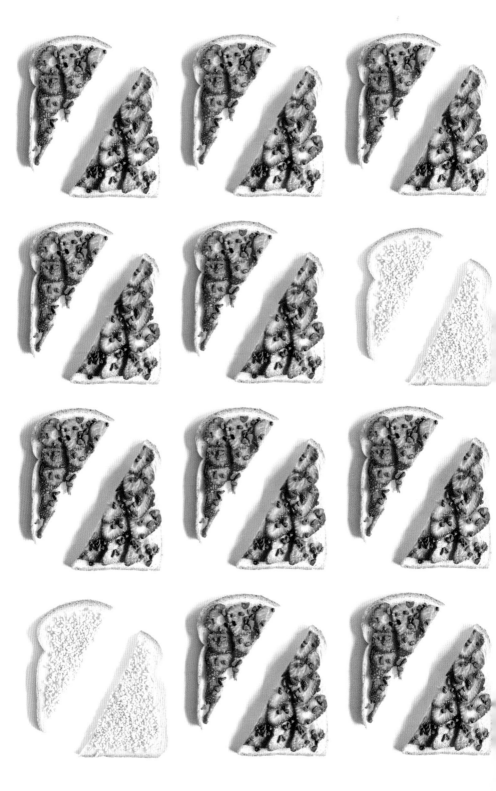

Enjoy life,
eat chocolate
sprinkles

Choco panna cotta

Preparation 30 minutes **Wait** 6 hours

6-8 servings

INGREDIENTS

5 GELATINE LEAVES
75 GR WHITE CHOCOLATE
75 GR DARK CHOCOLATE
450 GR FRESH WHIPPED CREAM
16 GR VANILLA SUGAR
9 TBSP HAGELSWAG (HAGELSLAG)
BAKING SPRAY

EXTRA

BOWL
2 HEAT RESISTANT BOWLS
2 SAUCEPANS
SILICON MOULDS (WE USED
DOME-LIKE MOULDS THE SIZE
OF A MUFFIN)

Soak 2½ gelatine leaves in a bowl with cold water. Melt the white chocolate au bain marie in a heat-resistant bowl. Meanwhile heat 225 gr cream and 8 gr vanilla sugar in a saucepan until it starts to boil. Remove the saucepan from the stove. Squeeze out the gelatine and add it to the cream. Once it has dissolved completely, mix in the melted chocolate. Spray the silicon mould with baking spray, add 1½ tbsp Hagelswag and fill the mould halfway with the chocolate mixture. Let it set for 3 hours in the fridge. Repeat the steps for the dark chocolate but leave out the Hagelswag this time. Pour this mixture on top of the white chocolate mixture and let it set for 3 hours.

Peach tiramisu

Preparation 20 minutes

4 servings

INGREDIENTS

16 SPONGE FINGERS
4 ESPRESSOS
60 ML TIA MARIA
100 ML CREAM
1 TIN OF PEACH HALVES IN SYRUP
1 TUB OF MASCARPONE
50 GR HAGELSLAG + EXTRA FOR
TOPPING

EXTRA

MIXER
MIXING BOWL

Soak the sponge fingers in a bath of espresso with Tia Maria. Once they are fully soaked, put 4 on a plate for each person. Mix the cream with the peach syrup and beat it together. The syrup should be added according to your taste. Then the mascarpone can be added. Once that has been fully mixed in, stir the hagelslag through it with a spoon. Cut the peaches into thin slices and cover the sponge fingers with them. Place a generous dollop of the mascarpone mix on top and sprinkle with some more hagelslag before serving.

Hot banana love

Preparation 5 minutes **Wait** 15 minutes

2 servings

INGREDIENTS

2 BANANAS

3 TBSP HAGELSLAG

4 TBSP RUM

EXTRA

GRILL OR BBQ

ALUMINIUM FOIL

Heat the grill or bbq. Put the bananas on a board and slice them from top to bottom keeping the bottom part intact. Gently push open the bananas and sprinkle in 1½ tbsp of hagelslag in each banana. Add 2 tbsp of rum in each banana and wrap them in aluminium foil. Close the package and place them on the grill for 15 minutes.

3

Spicy tomato soup

Preparation 15 minutes **Wait** 20 minutes

4-6 servings

INGREDIENTS

STOCK FROM 2 VEGETABLE STOCK CUBES

1 RED ONION

750 GR TOMATOES

2 PEPPERS

¾ CHILI PEPPER

1 TBSP OIL FOR BAKING

PINCH OF SALT AND PEPPER

4 TBSP HAGELSWAG (HAGELSLAG)

EXTRA

PAN

BLENDER

First bring 750 ml water to a boil. Add the stock cubes and stir in. Cut the onion into thin rings and the tomatoes into rough chunks. Remove the stalks from the tomatoes but keep the juice. Remove the pips from the peppers and cut into rough pieces. Finally cut the chili pepper into rough pieces, including the seeds. Heat the oil in a pan and fry the onion for a couple of minutes. Add the tomatoes, paprika and red pepper and stir well. Pour in the stock and allow to simmer for 20 minutes. Liquidise the soup in a blender. Add salt and pepper to taste. Stir in a tbsp of Hagelswag to each portion when serving.

Mushroom soup

Preparation 20 minutes

4 servings

INGREDIENTS

1 ONION
2 CLOVES OF GARLIC
2 TBSP OIL
250 GR CHESTNUT MUSHROOMS
250 GR WHITE MUSHROOMS
1 L VEGETABLE STOCK
200 GR CRÈME FRAÎCHE
PINCH OF SALT AND PEPPER
DASH OF SWEET SOY SAUCE
100 GR HAM STRIPS
4 TBSP HAGELSWAG (HAGELSLAG)

EXTRA

FRYING PAN
SAUCEPAN
BLENDER

Finely slice the onion and garlic finely and fry in the oil for a couple of minutes. Wipe all the mushrooms clean, and cut 300 gr into strips. Add to the frying pan and stir for 5 minutes. Add the vegetable stock and crème fraîche. Add salt and pepper to taste. Allow it to cook for another 10 minutes. In the meantime cut the remaining 200 gr of mushrooms into small cubes and bake them in the saucepan. Add a dash of sweet soy sauce. Have the 10 minutes passed? Blend the soup to a creamy mixture and finish off with the mushroom blocks. Serve on plates with a small spoon of crème fraîche and top it off with the ham strips and hagelslag.

Cauliflower risotto

Preparation 35 minutes

4 servings

INGREDIENTS

1 SMALL CAULIFLOWER

DASH OF OLIVE OIL

50 GR BUTTER

PINCH OF SALT

250 GR RISOTTO RICE

1 L STOCK

150 GR GRATED PARRANO CHEESE

1 TBSP COTTAGE CHEESE

4 TBSP DARK HAGELSLAG

40 GR PARMESAN CHEESE

CRESS

EXTRA

KITCHEN MACHINE

SMALL CUP

2 SAUCEPANS

Grind up the cauliflower in the kitchen machine. Take out a small cup of cauliflower and put it aside. Pour a dash of olive oil and 25 gr of butter into a saucepan. Add the remaining cauliflower and cook for a few minutes until hot. Add a pinch of salt. Melt 25 gr of butter in a large saucepan. Add the rice and keep stirring well. Once the rice grains become somewhat translucent you can add the stock. Do this 2-3 large spoons at a time, allowing the rice to absorb the stock before adding any more. Repeat this for about 20-25 minutes. Add the warm cauliflower mixture, grated parrano cheese and cottage cheese and stir well. Finally mix in the cup of raw cauliflower. Serve the risotto on a plate, making a well in the middle with a spoon. Fill this with a dessert spoon of hagelslag and decorate with Parmesan cheese and cress.

Flammkuchen

Preparation 10 minutes **Oven** 15-20 minutes

1 flammkuchen

INGREDIENTS

1 PACKAGE OF FRESH FLAMMKUCHEN DOUGH
140 GR CRÈME FRAÎCHE
1 ONION
100 GR GOAT'S CHEESE
PINCH OF PEPPER
40 GR ALMONDS
3 TBSP HAGELSLAG MIX MILK-WHITE

EXTRA

BAKING PAPER

Preheat the oven to 220°C. Cover a baking
tray with baking paper and cover with the
flammkuchen dough. Spread the crème fraîche
over the dough almost up to the edge. Fold
over the edges of the dough a little. Cut the
onion into thin rings. Spread the onion rings
and goat's cheese over the dough. Grind
the pepper over the goat's cheese. Bake the
flammkuchen in the oven for about 15 minutes.
Is the flammkuchen cooked and are the edges
nice and crispy? Chop the almonds up finely
and distribute the hagelslag mix and almonds
over the flammkuchen.

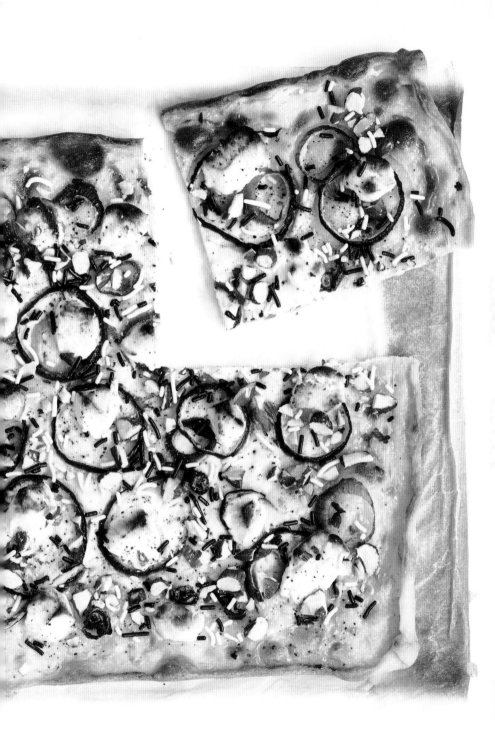

Leek onion pie

Preparation 25 minutes **Oven** 20 minutes

4 pies

INGREDIENTS

450 GR LEEKS
150 GR RED ONION
BAKING BUTTER
DASH OF SWEET SOY SAUCE
1 TSP THAI GREEN CURRY
1½ TSP RAS EL HANOUT
4 QUICHE PASTRY SHEETS
75 GR GORGONZOLA IN PIECES
4 TBSP WHITE CHOCOLATE
HAGELSLAG
40 GR PARMIGIANO REGGIANO

EXTRA

4 X Ø12 CM SPRINGFORM
FRYING PAN

Preheat the oven to 200°C. Cut the leeks and red onion into small pieces. Heat the butter in a saucepan. Add the leeks, onion and a dash of sweet soy sauce. Stir regularly and allow to gently simmer for about 10 minutes. Grease the springform baking pans. Spice up the mixture in the frying pan with the Thai green curry and ras el hanout to taste. Let the pastry thaw and put the sheets in the springforms, pressing them in a little. Stir the hagelslag and gorgonzola through the mixture and fill the springforms with it. Sprinkle grated Parmigiano Reggiano cheese over the pies and place them in the oven for 20 minutes. Delicious!

Gorgonzola **hagel** spaghetti

Preparation 20 minutes

2 servings

INGREDIENTS

250 GR CHESTNUT MUSHROOMS

DASH OF OLIVE OIL

200 GR SPINACH

150 GR SPAGHETTI

25 GR BUTTER

25 GR WHOLE GRAIN FLOUR

250 ML SEMI-SKIMMED MILK

PINCH OF PEPPER AND SALT

75 GR GORGONZOLA

2 TBSP DARK HAGELSLAG

1 HANDFUL WALNUTS

EXTRA

2 FRYING PANS

SAUCEPAN

Cut up the mushrooms and bake them in a pan with olive oil. Gradually add the spinach until everything has shrunk and then put aside. Cook the spaghetti according to the package instructions. Melt the butter in a saucepan and add the flour. Mix together well until smooth. Little by little add the milk, then add salt and pepper to taste. Mix in the mixture from the other pan, stirring well. Cut 40 gr gorgonzola into small pieces and stir through the mixture until melted. Then add the dark hagelslag and mix well. Serve the spaghetti and gorgonzola sauce on two plates. Garnish the plates with the remaining gorgonzola and walnuts.

Chocolate BBQ sauce

Preparation 15 minutes

1 large jar of sauce

INGREDIENTS

2 CLOVES OF GARLIC

2 TBSP BUTTER

1 SMALL ONION, SLICED FINELY

60 GR BROWN SUGAR

1 ESPRESSO

2 TBSP WHITE WINE VINEGAR

2 TBSP MUSTARD

2 TBSP WORCESTERSHIRE SAUCE

2 TSP CHILI POWDER

2 TSP SALT

2 TSP PEPPER

60 GR HAGELSWAG (HAGELSLAG)

EXTRA

SAUCEPAN

Cut the garlic into small pieces. Heat the butter in a pan and bake
the garlic and onion until they become golden. Add all remaining
ingredients and stir until hot. The sauce is ready to eat once the sugar
has melted. You can keep the sauce in the fridge for a couple of days
if it doesn't get eaten straight away.

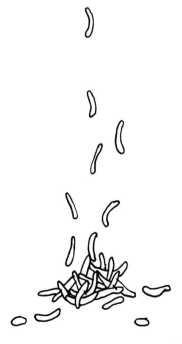

Chicken burger

Preparation 20 minutes

2 servings

INGREDIENTS

1 SHALLOT
1 CLOVE OF GARLIC
300 GR CHICKEN MINCE
1 TSP CHILI FLAKES
1½ TSP PORTUGESE CHICKEN HERBS
PINCH OF SALT AND PEPPER
1 EGG
5 TBSP BREADCUMBS
2½ TBSP HAGELSWAG (HAGELSLAG)
DASH OF OLIVE OIL

2 TASTY BURGER ROLLS
4 BACONSTRIPS
1 TOMATO
½ AVOCADO
LETTUCE

EXTRA

FRYING PAN
KITCHEN PAPER
MIXING BOWL

Cut the shallot and garlic up finely. Mix the chicken mince in a bowl with the shallot, garlic and herbs. Add the egg and gradually add the breadcrumbs, mixing well. Finally knead the Hagelswag into the mixture. Divide this into two burgers. If the burgers are too moist, add some extra breadcrumbs. Fry the burgers in the oil in a pan for about 8 minutes on both sides until nice and brown. Cut the tomato and avocado in slices. Serve the roll with the lettuce, tomato, avocado, burger and top it with the bacon.

Sticky **hagel** drumsticks

Preparation 10 minutes **Oven** 45 minutes **Wait** 30 minutes
4 drumsticks

INGREDIENTS
4 DRUMSTICKS
¾ RED PEPPER
1 CLOVE OF GARLIC
1½ TBSP OLIVE OIL
2 TBSP SOY SAUCE
3 TBSP HONEY
PINCH OF SEASONS PEPPER
2 TBSP DARK HAGELSLAG

EXTRA
BOWL
OVEN DISH

Cut the red pepper and garlic into very small pieces.
Mix the olive oil, soy sauce and honey in a bowl.
Add the red pepper, garlic, 4 seasons pepper and
hagelslag and mix well. Marinate the drumsticks with
this mixture and allow it to marinate for 30 minutes.
Preheat the oven to 180°C. Put the drumsticks in
an oven dish and cook in the oven for 45 minutes.
During this period turn the drumsticks 2 times and
pour the marinade over them.

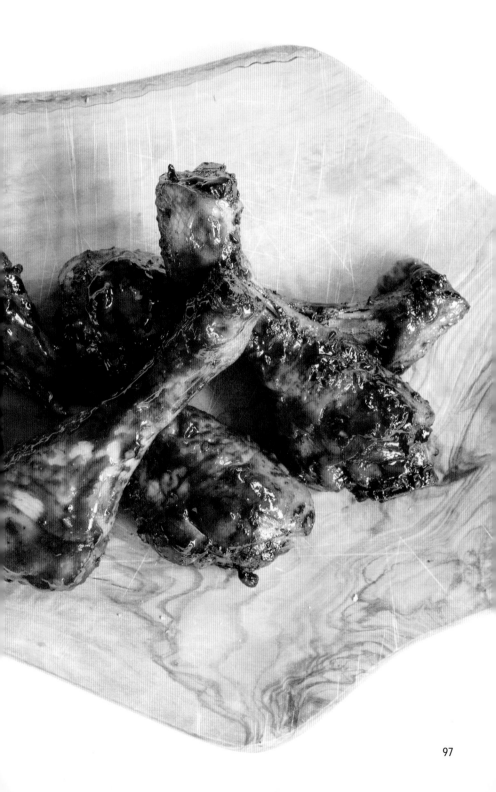

Milky **hagel**

Preparation 10 minutes

1 serving

INGREDIENTS

200 ML MILK

50 GR DARK CHOCOLATE

1 TSP COCOA

½ TSP CINNAMON

¼ TSP NUTMEG

¼ TSP SALT

¼ TSP CHILI POWDER OR FLAKES

DASH OF RUM (OPTIONAL)

TOPPING:

WHIPPED CREAM

½ TBSP HAGELSWAG (HAGELSLAG)

EXTRA

PAN

Heat all the ingredients (except the toppings) in a pan. Stir continually until the chocolate is completely melted. When all has melted and it begins to thicken, pour into a mug. If you like, you can add a dash of rum. Add a nice topping of whipped cream and sprinkle Hagelswag over it.

Cara-melt shake

Preparation 10 minutes

1 serving

INGREDIENTS

225 GR BUTTER

250 GR LIGHT BROWN SUGAR

150 ML WHIPPING CREAM

FOR THE SHAKE:

2 SCOOPS OF VANILLA ICE CREAM

200 ML MILK

3 TBSP CARAMEL

3 TBSP HAGELSLAG

WHIPPED CREAM AS TOPPING

EXTRA

SAUCEPAN

GLASS JAR

BOWL

GLASS

MIXER

Start by making the caramel: this can also be made upfront. Melt the butter in a saucepan with thick bottom. Add the sugar and cream and let it boil for a few minutes until the sugar has dissolved. Take the pan from the stove and pour the caramel into a glass jar. Let it cool. You can keep the caramel in the fridge.

Mix the ice cream, milk and 3 tbsp of home-made caramel. Add the hagelslag and pour it into a glass. Use some whipped cream as topping.

TIP Serve with a wide straw or long spoon.

Frost and hail

Preparation 5 minutes

1 serving

INGREDIENTS

15 ML ESPRESSO

15 ML WODKA

3 BAILEYS ICE CUBES

Pour the cold espresso and vodka together in a glass. Add three Baileys ice cubes and stir well. Drink once the ice cubes have melted.

MAKE BAILEYS ICE CUBES: Mix equivalent amounts of milk and Baileys together. Put some hagelslag into ice cube moulds and fill them up with the Baileys mixture. Then put the moulds into the freezer.

Choc fluff

Preparation 15 minutes

6 servings

INGREDIENTS

250 GR WHIPPED CREAM

2 TBSP GRANULATED SUGAR

1 TSP VANILLA EXTRACT

40 GR PEANUT BUTTER

60 ML MILK

100 GR MONCHOU/CREAM CHEESE

90 GR ICING SUGAR

30 GR HAGELSLAG

EXTRA

2 MIXING BOWLS

SPATULA

6 GLASSES

With a spatula, fold the whipped cream, granulated sugar and vanilla extract together in a bowl and put to the side. In another bowl mix the peanut butter, milk, monchou and icing sugar. Is it thoroughly mixed? Then fold the hagelslag through the mixture. Fill the 6 glasses halfway with the hagelslag mixture and top up with the whipped cream mix. Place the glasses in the fridge until you are ready to serve.

Confetti ice sandwich

Preparation 15 minutes **Wait** 90 minutes
16 servings

INGREDIENTS
225 GR BUTTER AT ROOM
TEMPERATURE
100 GR ICING SUGAR
100 GR WHITE CASTER SUGAR
250 GR FLOUR
1 TSP SALT
2 TSP VANILLA EXTRACT
60 GR HAGELSLAG MIX
60 GR COLOURED HAGELSLAG
1 L VANILLA ICE CREAM

EXTRA
MIXER
MIXING BOWL
SQUARE BAKING TIN
BAKING PAPER

Mix the butter with icing sugar and caster sugar. Add the flour, salt and vanilla extract. Once this is thoroughly mixed, add the hagelslag and knead it all together.

Split the pastry into two parts. Roll out one half and put it in a square baking tin covered with baking paper. Place the baking tin in the freezer and remove the ice cream from the freezer so that it can become a little softer. After about half an hour you can take the baking tin out of the freezer and spread the softened ice cream evenly over the first pastry layer. Return the baking tin to the freezer so the ice cream can harden. After about an hour the top pastry layer can be put on top. Keep in the freezer.

Gingerbread ice cream

Preparation 20 minutes **Wait** 2.5 hours
6 servings

INGREDIENTS
250 ML WHOLE MILK
70 GR WHITE DEMARERA SUGAR
4 EGG YOLKS
250 ML CREAM
150 GR GINGERBREAD IN SMALL
PIECES
70 GR HAGELSLAG

EXTRA
KITCHEN THERMOMETER
PAN
OVEN-PROOF BOWL
BOWL
DISH

Heat the milk au bain marie until it reaches 70°C. Mix the sugar and egg yolks in a bowl until smooth. Add this to the warm milk and heat until thickened. Once thickened, it can be cooled in the fridge. When fully cooled, beat the cream and add this, together with the gingerbread and hagelslag, to the cooled mixture. Thoroughly mix this all together and place, in a flat dish, in the freezer. During the first 2 hours, stir the ice every 20 minutes to prevent it from forming too many ice crystals, which would make the ice cream too hard.

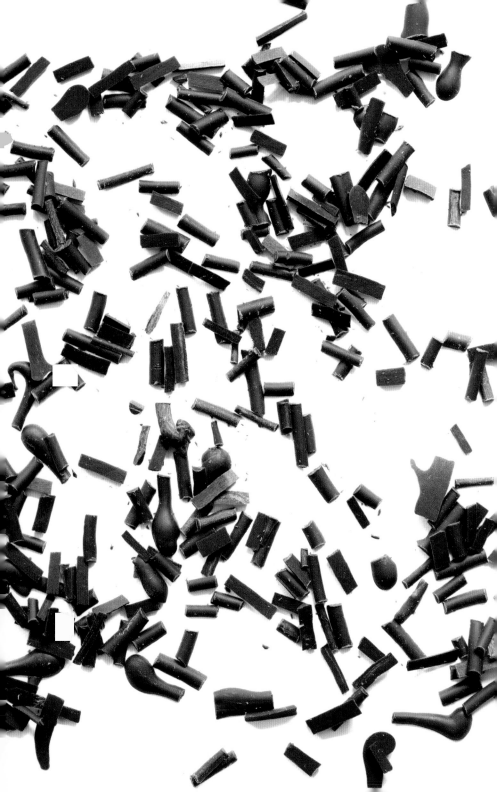

Hagel
around the world

Sprinkles are a traditional Dutch sandwich spread. Each country has its own traditional dishes, some of which also involve sprinkles.

Brigadeiros from Brazil are an example of this and should not be missed as a representative of dishes containing chocolate sprinkles. Or how about the Indonesian dish Pisang bakar coklat keju?

In addition to these familiar dishes, we have also introduced chocolate sprinkles as an additional ingredient in other traditional dishes. White sprinkles, for example, combine perfectly with smoked salmon and avocado on Danish smørrebrød. We introduce fusion cooking with sprinkles. Be creative, experiment and find your own favourite combination.

Scones

Preparation 15 minutes **Oven** 25 minutes

12 pieces

INGREDIENTS

250 GR SELF RISING FLOUR +
A LITTLE EXTRA FOR DUSTING
2½ TSP BAKING POWDER
1 TSP CINNAMON
½ TSP SALT
120 GR ICE-COLD BUTTER
80 GR MASCARPONE
40 GR CREAM + EXTRA FOR
BASTING
100 GR BROWN SUGAR
1 TSP VANILLA EXTRACT
1 EGG
120 GR HAGELSWAG (HAGELSLAG)
3 TBSP GRANULATED SUGAR

EXTRA

2 MIXING BOWLS
GRATER
BAKING PAPER

Preheat the oven to 200°C. Put the flour, baking powder, cinnamon and salt in a bowl and stir it all together. Grate the butter with a course grater and mix it through the dry ingredients with a fork. The mascarpone, cream, brown sugar, egg and vanilla essence should be mixed in another bowl. Pour this mixture into the first bowl and stir it together thoroughly. Finally mix in the Hagelswag. Make a ball out of the mixture and press it into a round plate, about 2.5 cm thick. Cut this into 10 pieces and place these at some distance from one another on the baking tray. Brush them with cream and sprinkle with granulated sugar. Slide the baking tray into the middle of the oven and bake the scones for 20-25 minutes. Let them cool a little before eating.

TIP Serve the scones with clotted cream.

Hagel pear strudel

Preparation 15 minutes **Oven** 50 minutes

10 servings

INGREDIENTS

1 PACK FILO PASTRY

1 KG PEARS

100 GR WHITE CASTER SUGAR

2 TBSP LEMON JUICE

70 GR WALNUTS

50 GR MELTED BUTTER

70 GR HAGELSLAG

EXTRA

FRYING PAN

BOWL

COLANDER

BAKING PAPER

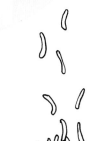

Take the filo pastry out of the freezer. Peel and core the pears and cut into small pieces. Sprinkle 50 gr of the sugar and the lemon juice over the pears. Roast the walnuts in a pan and cut them into small pieces. Preheat the oven to 180°C. Place a sheet of baking paper over a baking tray and cover this with sheets of filo pastry. Allow these to slightly overlap one another. Brush the sheets with some of the melted butter and sprinkle with 25 gr sugar.

Put another layer of filo pastry sheets on top and sprinkle the rest of the sugar on top. Spread the walnuts over the pastry. Drain the pear mixture in a colander and then distribute it across the pastry, but keep the edges free. Sprinkle the hagelslag across the top and then roll up into a roll, starting on a short side. You can use the baking paper to help you roll it in one go. Place the roll onto the baking paper on the baking tray and brush with the remaining melted butter. Bake the roll for 40-50 minutes in the oven. Delicious as a snack or as a dessert with a scoop of ice cream.

Brigadeiros

Preparation 20 minutes **Wait** 60 minutes
20 pieces

INGREDIENTS
1 TIN CONDENSED MILK
40 GR COCOA (SIEVED)
1 TBSP BUTTER + AN EXTRA TBSP
TO GREASE YOUR HANDS
BOWL WITH DARK HAGELSLAG

EXTRA
SAUCEPAN
PLATE

Put the condensed milk with cocoa and butter in a saucepan and mix well. Heat for about 10 minutes, stirring continuously. When the ingredients have formed one mass and it starts to come free from the edges you can remove the pan from the heat.
The mixture must then cool down for an hour in the fridge before it can be rolled into balls by hand. If you grease your hands with butter first you can easily form nice truffle-sized balls. Roll these through the hagelslag and your brigadeiro is ready!

Salmon smørrebrød

Preparation 5 minutes

1 serving

INGREDIENTS

1 SLICE OF RYE BREAD (60 GR)

1½ TSP CRÈME FRAÎCHE

HALF AN AVOCADO

40 GR SALMON

1 TBSP WHITE HAGELSLAG

Spread the crème fraîche onto the bread. Cut the avocado into slices and distribute these over the slice of bread. Arrange the salmon over this and top it off with hagelslag.

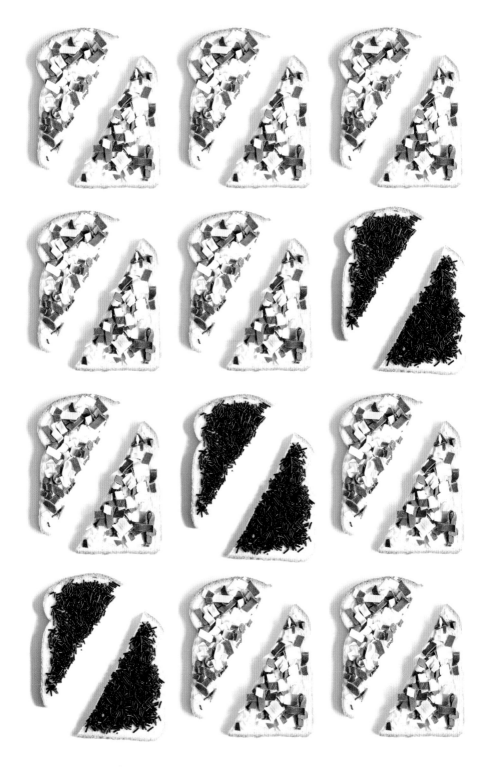

LET'S GO DUTCH AND EAT SOME HAGELSLAG

Brioche

Preparation 25 minutes **Oven** 35 minutes **Wait** 150 minutes

1 loaf

INGREDIENTS

375 GR FLOUR
50 GR SUGAR
6 GR DRIED YEAST
1 TSP SALT
60 GR MELTED BUTTER
115 ML LUKEWARM WATER
2 EGGS
1 EGG YOLK
120 GR HAGELSLAG
1 EGG WHITE

EXTRA

2 BOWLS
MIXER WITH A DOUGH
HOOK (OR HANDS)
TEA TOWEL
BAKING PAPER

Mix the flour, sugar, yeast and salt together in a bowl and make a well in it. In the other bowl mix together the melted butter, water, eggs and egg yolk. Gradually mix a small part of the wet mixture into the dry mixture, using the dough hook to knead it together (or you can use your hands). Knead for about 8 minutes to activate the yeast. If needed you can add a little flour. Grease a mixing bowl and put the ball of dough in it. Put this away in a warm place covered with a damp tea towel. The dough should become about twice its size in volume. This will take about 1.5 hours. Divide the dough into two equal pieces and roll one half into a flat rectangle on a countertop dusted with flour. Sprinkle 60 gr of the hagelslag over this and fold it lengthwise. Roll this into a long strand and divide this into two equal parts. Put these aside and repeat with the remaining dough. Plait the dough with the four strands to make a loaf. Keep moving the left-hand strand across the first strand to its right and the right-hand strand across two strands to its left. Put the loaf on a baking tray covered with baking paper and lay the damp tea towel over it. Leave this to rise again for an hour in a warm place. After an hour the tea towel can be removed and the loaf can be baked in a pre-heated oven at 190°C for about 35-40 minutes. It is ready when you can tap the bottom of the loaf and it sounds hollow.

TIP Serve the brioche with the **Hageldip cookie dough** on page 54.

American pancakes

Preparation 25 minutes

12-14 pancakes

INGREDIENTS

200 GR SELF-RAISING FLOUR
1½ TSP BAKING POWDER
1 TSP BROWN SUGAR
PINCH OF SALT
3 EGGS
25 GR MELTED BUTTER + EXTRA
FOR BAKING
200 ML MILK
70 GR HAGELSWAG (HAGELSLAG)

TOPPING:
MAPLE SYRUP
HAGELSWAG (HAGELSLAG)
BLUEBERRIES
EDIBLE FLOWERS

EXTRA

MIXING BOWL
MIXER OR WHISK
FRYING PAN

Mix the flour, baking powder, brown sugar and salt in a bowl. Make a well in the middle using the back of a spoon. Add the eggs, melted butter and milk to the well. Mix this thoroughly with a mixer until it becomes a nice smooth batter, and then pour into a jug.

Heat a lump of butter in a frying pan. Once the butter is warm, pour some batter into the pan to form a pancake of about 8 cm wide.

If you are baking more than one pancake at once in the pan, make sure you don't pour them too close together, as they might stick together.

Bake them for 2-3 minutes until many small bubbles appear on the surface. Flip the pancake and bake the other side for 2-3 minutes.

Repeat until the batter has been used up.

Top the pancakes off with maple syrup, hagelslag, blueberries and (optional) edible flowers.

Bread pudding

Preparation 10 minutes **Oven** 25 minutes

2 servings

INGREDIENTS
90 ML MILK
2 EGGS
2 TBSP SUGAR
½ TSP VANILLA EXTRACT
3-4 SLICES OF WHITE BREAD
2 TBSP HAGELSLAG
BAKING SPRAY

EXTRA
MIXING BOWL
2 OVEN-PROOF MUGS

Preheat the oven to 180°C. Mix the milk, eggs, sugar and vanilla extract in a bowl. Cut the bread into 2 x 2 cm squares and add these to the mixture. Make sure the bread is thoroughly mixed in. Stir in the hagelslag. Spray the mugs and then fill them with the mixture. Place the mugs in the preheated oven for 25 minutes. Eat them whilst still warm. A delicious breakfast or special dessert.

Pisang bakar coklat keju

Preparation 10 minutes

2 servings

INGREDIENTS

2 BANANAS
BUTTER
GRATED CHEESE TO TASTE
HAGELSLAG TO TASTE

EXTRA

FRYING PAN

Cut the bananas in two, lengthwise.
Melt a lump of butter in a fryingpan on
the stove. When the pan is fully hot add
the halved bananas. Turn the bananas
after about 4 minutes and let the other
side caramelise for about 3 minutes.
Share the bananas across two plates and
sprinkle generously with the cheese and
hagelslag.
Eat while the bananas are still hot.

Chili con carne

Preparation 15 minutes **Wait** 25 minutes
4 servings

INGREDIENTS

1½ PEPPERS
1 CLOVE OF GARLIC
1 ONION
DASH OF OLIVE OIL
300 GR MINCED MEAT
2 TSP PAPRIKA POWDER
2 TSP GROUND CUMIN
2 TSP SAMBAL
PINCH OF SALT AND PEPPER
2½ TBSP TOMATO PUREE
100 ML STOCK
400 GR KIDNEY BEANS
350 GR BAKED BEANS WITH ITS
SAUCE
3 TBSP HAGELSLAG

EXTRA

LARGE PAN

Cut the pepper into small cubes and put aside. Slice up the garlic and onion finely, and fry this in a large pan with some olive oil. Add the mince and break it up whilst stirring, until cooked brown. Add the paprika, cumin, sambal, salt, pepper and tomato puree and cook together for another minute. Add the cubed peppers and stock. Let the mixture simmer for 15 minutes. Then add the drained kidney beans and baked beans in their sauce, and allow this to continue simmering for a further 10 minutes. Finally stir the hagelslag through the chili con carne.

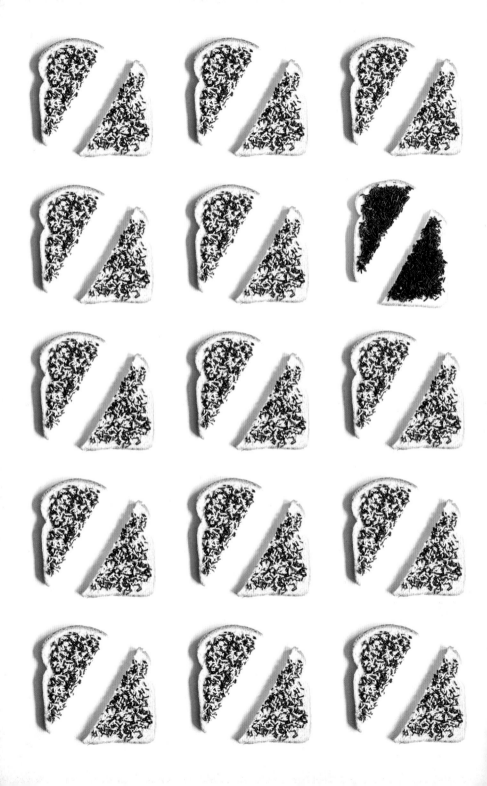

SPREAD
THE HAGEL

Word of thanks

Our third book for Scriptum was again a fantastic collaboration. Tosca and Gerjan, thanks so much for giving us the opportunity to create a book as we envision it. And for the first time an English-language version! Eveline, Gabina, Thea and Bram, thank you for your help and promotion of our book.

Dieteke and Marieke, thank you very much for your help in the kitchen and for lending us your thinking cap. You have really been a wonderful help. Marieke and David, thank you very much for translating our recipes into English. This is greatly appreciated and very helpful. Hans, sorry for all the chaos and extra pounds. Thank you so much for being our test person again and also for your generosity in sharing your refrigerator and freezer with Cookart. Friends, colleagues and housemates, thank you for helping us eat all the dishes and thank you for your feedback on all dishes. Olaf (www.olafschouw.com), thank you for the beautiful pictures you made of us and the Hagelswag men. Robbert and Lennart, thank you for this wonderful cooperation. With this book we hope to show people that it is not just Hagelswag for breakfast, but **Hagelswag always!**

About the **authors**

Jennifer Foster and Lianne Koster work together as Studio Cookart, where they can combine their passion for good food and for creating something beautiful. Since 2015 they have regularly been found lying on the ground taking pictures, as well as annoying the neighbours with their singing – and they are not afraid to tell each other what they think of something. Lianne has long had a reputation as a nit-picker and Jennifer has to be held back regularly when it comes to her choice of crazy words – some of which have found their way into this book.

Despite the hectic, wild and irregular days, they find their peace around 11 o'clock by cuddling with mascot Afrodite (tortoise) and at 2 o'clock (early 4 o'clock for them) with a can of diet coke. Working out is no longer necessary on their working days. With their fantastic playlists they challenge each other to come up with the best moves. A dance or a pistol squat, nothing is too hard for them. Sometimes they allow themselves to become distracted – with chocolate sprinkles left out of the recipe as a result. But it has all turned out great. The chocolate sprinkles book is a fact. **Spread the hagel!**

INDEX

HET
PINDAKAASBOEK

Jennifer Foster & Lianne Koster

SCRIPTUM

Flexicover, 14,5 x 21 cm • 144 pages, fullcolour
ISBN 978 94 6319 048 0